How to Do Homework Without Throwing Up

By
Written & illustrated by Trevor Romain
Edited by Elizabeth Verdick

EasyRead Large

Copyright Page from the Original Book

Library of Congress Cataloging-in-Publication Data
Romain, Trevor.
    How to do homework without throwing up / written and illustrated by Trevor Romain ; edited by Elizabeth Verdick.
      p. cm.
    Summary: Discusses a variety of simple techniques for getting homework done.
    ISBN 1-57542-011-2
    1. Homework—Juvenile literature. [1. Homework.] I. Verdick, Elizabeth. II. Title.
LB1048.R59 1997.
371.3′028′1—dc21   96–47405

Cover art by Trevor Romain

Cover and text design by MacLean & Tuminelly

Printed on recycled paper
including 30%
post-consumer waste

20 19 18 17 16 15 14 13 12
Printed in the United States of America

Free Spirit Publishing Inc.
217 Fifth Avenue North, Suite 200
Minneapolis, MN 55401-1299
(612) 338-2068
help4kids@freespirit.com
www.freespirit.com

Free Spirit Publishing is a member of the Green Press Initiative, and we're committed to printing our books on recycled paper containing a minimum of 30% post-consumer waste (PCW). For every ton of books printed on 30% PCW recycled paper, we save 5.1 trees, 2,100 gallons of water, 114 gallons of oil, 18 pounds of air pollution, 1,230 kilowatt hours of energy, and .9 cubic yards of landfill space. At Free Spirit it's our goal to nurture not only young people, but nature too!

green press INITIATIVE

TABLE OF CONTENTS

"A great little paperback for parents and educators
to share with those who think homework
is the bane of childhood."

—School Library Journal

Read, America! Selection

Dedication

For Michael Thompson, who does not let
cancer stop him from doing his homework.
Also for Steve, Chesney, and Mauro,
the homework experts of my childhood.

Do not read this!

You peeked!
Ha! Now that I have your attention—
I must tell you that this book
is about homework. That's right...

HOMEWORK

Before you say, "Homework, who needs it?"
think
again. You need it, my friend. It's not just there
to make your life miserable. (Image 1.1)

Image 1.1

Here are a few good reasons for doing
homework:

- It helps you practice skills that you haven't fully learned yet. And it helps you review skills that you have learned.

- It gives you the chance to finish up tasks that you couldn't get done during school hours.

- It helps you to learn and grow.

Now, repeat after me:

"Homework is not horrible." (Well, not that horrible.)

"I can do my homework **WITHOUT THROWING UP!**"

Everybody who goes to school does homework. You are not alone. And they feel just as sick as you do when they have to do it. (Image 1.2)

Image 1.2

Image 1.3

Hanging out instead of going home and doing your homework is called *procrastinating.* Procrastinating means: I'll think of a thousand things to do to keep me from doing my homework. (Image 1.3)

Image 1.4

Do not pull your hair out because you have homework to do. (The homework won't get done, and you'll go bald.) (Image 1.4)

Image 1.5

People who say homework is a waste of time don't know what they're talking about. They'll probably grow up without useful skills and might end up with jobs they really don't like. (Image 1.5)

Image 1.6

Throwing a fit will not make your homework easier to do. It will probably just get you grounded! (Image 1.6)

You cannot make your homework disappear! It will not vanish into thin air. If you try to get rid of your homework, it will just come back the next day to haunt you. (Image 1.7)

Image 1.7

Image 1.8

You cannot escape homework. It will follow you wherever you go. Even to the North Pole. Get to your homework before it gets to you. (Image 1.8)

Do not fight or argue with your homework! You will lose. The best way to get your homework done without feeling sick every time you see it is to *just do it.* (Image 1.9)

In fact, if you have any homework at the moment, put this book down and go do it. You'll feel great afterwards, and you'll be able to enjoy what you're reading without having that nagging "Uh-oh, gotta do my homework" feeling in the back of your mind.

Image 1.9

Image 1.10

Do not blame the contents of your room for your homework. Breaking your pencil into a thousand pieces, kicking your desk, attacking the lamp, or yelling at your teddy bear will **NOT** make your homework do itself. **YOU** must do it. (Image 1.10)

Although you pray as hard as you can pray,
wish as hard as you can wish,
cry as hard as you can cry,
HOMEWORK HAPPENS! (Image 1.11)

Image 1.11

Ten Terrible Excuses for Not Doing Your Homework:

Image 1.12

1. I don't feel like it.

2. No time.

3. Homework? What homework?

4. I left it at school, on the bus, in the cafeteria....

5. I have to watch my favorite TV show.

6. Nobody reminded me.

7. Homework is really, really, really, really BOR-ing.

8. I have better things to do.

9. I didn't write down the assignment.

10. My dog might eat it.

Here's a **GREAT** thing about homework. You get to do it at home! (Image 1.13)

Image 1.13

Image 1.14

Try to make friends with your homework. Friends are a lot easier to deal with than enemies. (Image 1.14)

Make a homework schedule. This will tell you exactly when to do your homework and when to do all the really fun stuff that keeps you from doing homework.

Hang your schedule on the fridge or in your room so you don't forget about it. (**TIP:** Do not crumple, mangle, spit on, sneeze on, throw up on, wipe your dirty fingers on, or tear your homework schedule into a million pieces!) (Image 1.15 & 1.16)

Image 1.15

Image 1.16

The D (for Duh) Homework Schedule

4:00 to 7:30	Play outdoors, feed the dog, eat dinner, play video games, feed goldfish, read comic book, pick nose, twiddle thumbs, stare at the ceiling for the longest time.
7:30 to 9:30	Do it all again and watch TV.
9:30	Go to bed.
9:31	Stare at the ceiling again, remember big major homework assignment you didn't do, sweat profusely, bite fingernails, wish for a flood or other disaster to happen so you won't have to go to school tomorrow.

Table 1.1

The A+ Homework Schedule

Image 1.17

4:00 to 4:30	Play outdoors, have a quick and healthy snack.

4:30 to 5:30	Homework Time! Breathe deeply, do homework, think hard, stretch, think harder.
5:30 to 7:00	Stop homework, play, feed dog, call a friend, eat dinner.
7:00 to 8:00	Finish up any remaining homework.
8:00 to 9:30	Free Time (if your homework is done).
9:30	Go to bed, sleep like a baby, dream about how happy your teacher will be about your completed homework!

Table 1.2

Image 1.18

Find a homework helper. Get a good friend, or a parent or relative, to help you with your homework. A homework helper will help you to understand things. (Image 1.18)

Image 1.19

Try to eat something before you do your homework. It's easier to concentrate if you're not thinking about food.

NOTE: Eating the back of your pencil while doing your homework is not good for your gums. Plus, you get gross flecks of yellow stuff stuck between your teeth. (Image 1.19)

Image 1.20

FOOD FOR THOUGHT: Your brain needs fuel to run on. Foods high in proteins, carbohydrates, and vitamins can provide that fuel. Foods high in fat weigh you down. Fats are hard to digest, so they keep blood in the stomach area and not in the brain (where you want it!). (Image 1.20)

Feed your brain healthy snacks and drink a glass of water, juice, or milk. Caffeinated drinks like soda will energize you for a little while, but then you'll just feel more tired later. (Image 1.21)

Image 1.21

Great Pre-Homework Snacks (for energy):

- Peanut butter and jelly sandwich
- Carrots and celery
- Granola bar
- Fruit
- Popcorn
- Yogurt (Image 1.22)

Image 1.22

Not-So-Great Pre-Homework Snacks:

- Two candy bars
- A handful of chocolate chip cookies
- A double bacon cheeseburger and fries
- Leftover candy from last Halloween
- Super-Duper-Sugar brand cereal

- An entire bag of potato chips (Image 1.23)

- A high-caffeine soft drink

Image 1.23

Before you do your homework, try to clear your head. Spend a few seconds breathing deeply, and push interfering thoughts out of your mind. (Image 1.24)

Image 1.24

Image 1.25

Pick the hardest homework and do it first. Save the easiest for last. This means the more you do your homework, the easier it gets. (Image 1.25)

Do your homework in the same place every day. This way, the minute you sit down, you automatically switch into homework mode. As time goes by, this will become a routine and doing your homework will become easier. (Image 1.26)

Image 1.26

Image 1.27

You cannot watch television and do your homework at the same time. It doesn't work!

People who do their homework while watching television often develop "TV-Homework-Neck" (a nervous twitch-of-the-head that occurs as a result of continually flicking your head up to get a quick look at the television as you work. The more you flick, the more you twitch. The more you twitch, the more you flick). (Image 1.27)

This terrible condition gets worse as you age. "TV-Homework-Neck" is embarrassing when you get old enough to kiss and you keep missing the other person's mouth.

Image 1.28

Homework has a **SPEED LIMIT!** Do not write faster than 55 miles per hour. If you do your homework at excessive speeds, you'll miss turns, hit bumps, and lose your way. (And your pencil might burst into flames.) (Image 1.28)

If noise bothers you while you do your homework, tell everyone in the house to **PLEASE BE QUIET!** If they don't listen, call a family meeting and say, "Hey, I am a responsible student. I am dedicated to furthering my education. I am determined to be somebody. So ... please **HUSH** for goodness sake!" (Image 1.29)

Image 1.29

Image 1.30

Sometimes it helps to have a little intermission while you're doing your homework. Little breaks during homework help to refresh your mind. (Image 1.30)

When I say little break, I mean a **LITTLE** break of five minutes. Not a four hour break that includes three television shows, a basketball game, two pieces of toast, teasing the neighbor's dog, reading all your comic books, and playing video games.

Avoid picking your nose or pulling out your eyebrow hairs while doing homework. This will only distract you. (Image 1.31)

Image 1.31

Image 1.32

Homework can be useful! If you want something from your parents, the best way to get it is to use your completed homework as a tool. To make this work really well for you, use the words, "I've done my homework," after every sentence. For effective results, always drop your voice when you say "done my homework." For example: "Mom, I need the new X-Men comic book. I've done my homework. And the store down the street has those comics. I've done my homework. Can you drive me there because I have ... done my homework." (Image 1.32)

Doing your homework makes parents very happy. A happy parent will make you happy, and a happy you will make your homework easier to do.

Image 1.33

Sometimes kids have a problem with homework because they simply can't see what's on the blackboard. If you have trouble seeing what the teacher is writing, you might need glasses. (When I was young, I had a problem with homework until my mother took me to the eye doctor. My whole life changed when I started wearing glasses. I could see!) (Image 1.33)

Participating in class makes homework easier to do because the more involved you get, the better you'll understand what you're being taught. (Image 1.34)

Image 1.34

Image 1.35

In class, think for yourself. If you keep asking other people for the answers, you won't understand the material and your homework will be hard to complete. (Image 1.35)

If you sleep in class, you won't even know that you have homework to do! (Image 1.36)

Image 1.36

Image 1.37

Feeling down... (Image 1.37)

...or depressed about your homework means you need help. Ask your teacher or parent for help. They might suggest that you get a tutor. A tutor can teach you things you're having trouble understanding and will help you sharpen your skills. Don't be afraid to get a tutor. (Image 1.38)

Image 1.38

Image 1.39

Once you've received the help you need, you'll feel **A LOT** better about your homework and about yourself. (Image 1.39)

Drinking alcohol or using drugs does **NOT** make homework easier to do. It just makes you a dope! (Image 1.40)

Image 1.40

Image 1.41

You shouldn't fear your homework. Your homework should fear **YOU!** (Simply because you can take care of your homework anytime you want to.) (Image 1.41)

Your teacher didn't invent homework, so don't try to make your teacher's life miserable. For example, do **NOT** stick a big piece of gooey chewed-up bubblegum on your teacher's chair! (Image 1.42)

Image 1.42

Image 1.43

You cannot bribe your teacher with an apple or even homemade apple pie. (Bribing means giving your teacher a gift so that he or she will not give you homework.) Don't even try it! (Image 1.43)

If the sight of your homework makes you want to puke, let your teacher know. Say, "Sir or Ma'am, I'm going to throw up all over this homework because I don't understand it. I feel green, I have a headache, and I'm afraid I'm going to fail. I need some help, please." (Image 1.44)

Image 1.44

Image 1.45

Believe it or not, most teachers will not yell at you or make you feel stupid. Your teacher will **HELP** you. That's why your teacher is there. (Image 1.45)

NO! Your teacher will not believe the toilet ate your homework. (Image 1.46)

Image 1.46

Image 1.47

And your teacher will not believe the dog ate your homework either. **DOGS DO NOT EAT HOMEWORK!** A dog will throw up if it tries to eat any type of homework, especially if it's a science project. (Image 1.47)

Turn your homework into a good habit, like brushing your teeth. Soon you won't even know you're doing it. (Image 1.48)

Image 1.48

Secret Advice!

Image 1.49

Reading makes homework a lot easier to do. The more you read, the better you'll understand things. It's quite amazing. Without even knowing it, you'll get smarter. Reading opens your mind like a key opens a lock. It's automatic! (Image 1.49)

For practice, read anything and everything: great literature, poems, novels, nonfiction, plays, short stories, mysteries, magazines, newspapers, journals, your big sister's diary (**OOPS!** Just kidding!), maps, comic books, road signs, billboards, cereal boxes—the list goes on and on! (Image 1.50)

Image 1.50

Image 1.51

A great thing about finishing your homework is that you'll have free time to spend with your friends and family—without that nagging "Uh-oh, gotta do my homework" feeling. After you've worked so hard, you'll have a great time watching a movie, having a picnic, going out for dinner, or spending the rest of the day doing things you love to do. (Image 1.51)

WARNING! Homework has serious side effects. You might become smart and successful if you do all your homework! (Image 1.52)

Image 1.52

You'll not only feel relieved when you complete your homework, but you'll also feel proud. Being proud of what you do boosts your self-esteem. So, doing a good job on your homework can actually make you feel great about your accomplishments and yourself all at the same time. (Image 1.53)

Image 1.53

Quick Reminders:

- Do your homework in the same place every time. Make sure it's a quiet place with the TV off.

- Eat a meal or light snack before doing your homework. (Image 1.54)

Image 1.54

- Do the hardest assignment first.

- Find a homework helper, if you need one. This can be a good friend, a classmate, or a parent. (Your goldfish cannot be a homework helper.) (Image 1.55)

Image 1.55

- Ask your teacher for help when you need it. (**TIP:** Do this while you're still at school. Desperately telephoning your teacher at midnight is **NOT** a good idea.) (Image 1.56)

Image 1.56

- Ask your family to respect your homework time. If you want, put a "Do Not Disturb" sign on your door (or on your forehead). (Image 1.57)

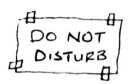

Image 1.57

- Take little breaks during your homework time. Stand up and stretch, get a drink of water or an energizing snack, or do ten jumping jacks—whatever keeps you going. (Image 1.58)

Image 1.58

Five Homework Gripes (and what to do about 'em!):

1. "I don't have time." (*Make* time. Remember this: Homework is not optional!) (Image 1.59)

Image 1.59

Image 1.60

2. "I don't understand it." (Ask your teacher for help before the school day is over. Do all the parts you can do, then figure out

where you're stuck. At home, do not be afraid to ask an adult or your older brother or sister to help you.) (Image 1.60)

Image 1.61

3. "I can't ever finish it." (Find out why. Are you distracted? Are you having trouble in a certain subject? Ask your teacher or a parent for some advice about managing your time.) (Image 1.61)

4. "I have too much homework." (Organize yourself. Make a homework schedule that says what you'll do and when you'll do it. Use a calendar to remind yourself of short-term and long-term assignments. Do not procrastinate! Ask your teacher to give you advance notice of upcoming projects

so you can get an early start.) (Image 1.62)

Image 1.62

Image 1.63

5. "I forget to bring my books home." (Remind yourself each day before you leave school to do a "Backpack Check." Do you have everything you need? Write little

reminders to yourself on your notebooks, in your locker, on your hand—whatever works for you.) (Image 1.63)

The nicest thing about doing your homework is the feeling you get when it's **DONE!** (Image 1.64)

Image 1.64

Image 1.65

Doing your homework to the best of your ability will one day help you to reach as high as you can reach and go as far as you want to go! (Image 1.65)

About the Author/Illustrator

Image I

When South African-born Trevor Romain was 12, his teacher told him he wasn't talented enough to do art. By accident, he found out 20 years later that he could draw. Since that lucky day, he has written and illustrated more than 30 books for children and created an animated video series for kids based on his best-selling, award-winning books. In addition to writing, illustrating, drinking tea, and trying to avoid trouble, Trevor regularly visits schools to speak to children, and he spends his free time with kids who have cancer at the Brackenridge Hospital in Austin, Texas. Trevor receives hundreds of letters annually from principals, teachers, and students who have been touched by his humor and energy.

***

To place an order or to request a free catalog of SELF-HELP FOR KIDS® and SELF-HELP FOR TEENS® materials,
please write, call, email, or visit our Web site:

Free Spirit Publishing Inc.
217 Fifth Avenue North • Suite 200
• Minneapolis, MN 55401-1299
toll-free 800.735.7323 • local 612.338.2068
• fax 612.337.5050
help4kids@freespirit.com
• www.freespirit.com

Back Cover Material

DO NOT read this book if you love doing

HOMEWORK

But if homework makes you uneasy or queasy, this book is for you. Author Trevor Romain understands how horrible homework can be. And he knows how you can do yours without throwing up. As you laugh along with Trevor's jokes and cartoons, you'll learn important homework truths, like:

- Though it might feel good at the time, throwing a fit will not make your homework easier to do.

- Dogs do not eat homework, especially science projects.

You'll also learn valuable homework skills, like:

- how to make a homework schedule,

- how to get help with your homework, and

- how to avoid TV-Homework-Neck.

So don't avoid this book (it's NOT your homework). Read it. Try the ideas in it. They really work!

Trevor Romain has written and illustrated many books for children. In addition to writing and illustrating, Trevor also spends a lot of time with children who are ill. He is a board member of the Candlelighters Childhood Cancer Foundation and can often be found on the cancer ward of Children's Hospital at Brackenridge Hospital in Austin, Texas, doing his rounds as "Doctor of Mischief."

A *Read, America!* Selection

free spirit PUBLISHING®

Helping kids
help themselves™
since 1983

www.freespirit.com

Books For ALL Kinds of Readers

At ReadHowYouWant we understand that one size does not fit all types of readers. Our innovative, patent pending technology allows us to design new formats to make reading easier and more enjoyable for you. This helps improve your speed of reading and your comprehension. Our EasyRead printed books have been optimized to improve word recognition, ease eye tracking by adjusting word and line spacing as well as minimizing hyphenation. Our EasyRead SuperLarge editions have been developed to make reading easier and more accessible for vision-impaired readers. We offer Braille and DAISY formats of our books and all popular E-Book formats.

We are continually introducing new formats based upon research and reader preferences. Visit our web-site to see all of our formats and learn how you can Personalize our books for yourself or as gifts. Sign up to Become A (RHYW) Registered Reader.

www.readhowyouwant.com